Spring Haze

adam gibson

BookLeaf Publishing

India | USA | UK

Presentation by *BookLeaf Publishing*

Web: www.bookleafpub.com

E-mail: info@bookleafpub.com

ISBN: 9789358735659

First edition 2023

*This book is dedicated to my wife and
family, who I love dearly.*

ACKNOWLEDGEMENT

To Percy Bysshe Shelley and Tori Amos, without them I may have never found the inspiration to keep writing. My rebel spirit was at least partly due to reading about Percy Bysshe Shelley at a young age.

PREFACE

These poems were written by me. Each poem has captured a piece of my soul. I have never written for anyone else, and therefore you may not understand or appreciate where these poems come from. That is fine, just know that each poem in this collection is authentic. My love of people and nature has shaped these poems. Even though they may seem dark at times, they do come from a place of happiness and light. I hope they make you think and feel as you read them. If you can get something out of them, I will be happy. Enjoy!

10 days before Christmas

10 days before Christmas my story begins
Without shiny reindeer or fat jolly men
This story it start in the city on streets
Far removed from the happiness, other stories do
preach
No white Christmas, No elves and not even St
Nick
Just a couple of addicts, lost, alone and sick
Making their money sucking on sticks
I'm not trying to be crass, just telling what I see
In this crystal ball, the story presents itself to me

Michael, the old boy, was the star of the show
Until he caught a disease, shooting up blow
And now only has a year or so….to go
The sad girl Sally, started out as his wife
Until he showed her the edge of his knife
And couldn't live with the decisions that created
this life

Divorced they both drifted away from their love
But ended up on the same street, both strung out
on drugs
They compete for the tricks that will give them
their fix

The story is sad, but it has a nice twist

Their daughter was born, but raised far away
The Child Welfare department got one right on
that day
She grew up in Seattle, in a nice suburban home
The parents that raised her made sure she would
never be alone
She had an older brother; he was adopted just
the same
And also a younger sister who was born to their
family name
The family was quite happy, many presents
under the tree
The girl named Daisy was as happy as could be

For 18 years Daisy believed she was a true born
daughter
Until one fateful night when the news was
sprung upon her
It happened rather frankly by a distant cousin
girl
Who didn't realize she held the knowledge that
would change 3 worlds
The family was looking at pictures, when the
subject of babies came
This older cousin, started to recall the wonderful
adoption day

She spoke of how the baby girl, arrived with so
much curly blondish hair
And looked so much like her adoptive mother, it
was hard to believe they weren't a pair
Daisy's mind went blank; she could hear the
silence crack
Her life changed in that instance, there was no
going back

That night, she barely slept a wink
So many thoughts filled her head, it was hard to
think
When she woke the next morning, she knew
what she had to do
She had to find her true born parents; she had to
find the truth

Her search began at the clinic; it wasn't that hard
to find a name
But once she had that info, inside she didn't feel
the same
The last name was different than the one she'd
always known
It made her feel adopted, for the first time she
felt alone
She found the last address that her parents did
share
And made the decision, to board a plane and
travel there

But when she arrived at the doorstep, she found
the house condemned
The windows were all boarded, the fence posts
all upended
She sat on the stairs, as the tears started to flow
Wondering if her journey had ended, if the truth
would ever be known
She thought about going back to Seattle, where
she knew she was missed
But inside she felt needed, like this journey
would bring bliss
She asked all of the neighbors, and was directed
to a street
With a warning to go away, for these people she
shouldn't meet
"Go back home, little girl", "Don't get involved
in their shame"
"This isn't the life for you", "Stay away! Stay
away!"
But Daisy was determined; she had to find the
truth
And traveled to the corner to find her parents, to
share the news
That she was their daughter and to offer them
her love
Forgiveness she would utter and shower them
with hugs

When she got to the street corner, she asked
around and was told
That her father was in the hospital, her mother
was sleeping in the cold
She was guided to an alley, a dirty mattress on
the ground
A homeless woman sleeping, her mother was
finally found
It was hard for Daisy to see this; she wanted to
help in some way
And tried to wake her mother, but was told "Go
Away!"
Daisy tried to explain the situation; she said
"I'm your daughter, yes its me!"
But the women didn't want to hear this, she just
kicked and screamed
Daisy tried her best to tell her, she tried so hard
to explain
But the woman had forgotten, all she knew now
was the pain
Daisy gave her a little money, wrote her number
with a pen
Told her to contact her if she ever needed a
friend

To the hospital she walked, maybe her father
would be more kind
But when she walked through the doors, she
leaned this man just had died

Daisy couldn't think straight, something was
amiss
Then she noticed the day, the eve of Christmas
and she was apart from the family that loves her,
She realizes she had everything, she didn't need
another mother
She went to the airport, boarded a plane and
made it home
When she opened the door, she no longer felt
alone

She learned a valuable lesson that family isn't in
your blood
The people that matter most are those that raise
you with love

Growing Up

From lands far and lands wide
there is a strange tale
of a heroic boy named Cal
his adventures inspired this fable

Cal was a young lad
from Ireland, green
He wasn't much older
than the children that are seen
on playgrounds, in school
playing with toys
But Cal was much different
than those girls and boys

Cal had a secret
that no one else knew
His friends were all fairies
of yellow, pink and blue
He preferred their kind company
to the taunting and teasing
of the young boys and girls
that were much less than pleasing

one quiet summer morning
when most were asleep

his adventure began
as he heard a soft weep
"why are you crying"
"what can I do?"
blue fairy replied
"Im crying for you"

"What have I done"
Cal asked with concern
"It not what you have done,
but what you will learn"

Confused, empathetic
Cal sat on the ground
next to the blue fairy
and said "your words please expound"
blue fairy stood up
"do you really want to know"
Cal smiled and uttered
"Yes, I want you to show"

So quick as a rabbit
slick as a sleuth
The lights all went dark
and exposed was the truth

the future revealed
Cal, now a young man
who was wealthy, not wanting

gold rings on his hand

He lived in a mansion
with 300 rooms
more money than kings
Im sure to assume

He laughed like a tyrant
at the poor gentle knaves
100 little fairies
all digging their own graves

Cal, cried as he watched
what one day would become
"what happened to me
where is all my love"

blue fairy smiled softly
and spoke with a sadness
"You revealed our secret
and soon moral badness
took over your soul
with riches and such
you couldnt resist
their temptation was too much"

"when does this happen?
how can I change"
"The wheels are set in motion"

blue fairy explained

"Theres nothing you can do,
nothing left to say"
blue fairy kissed Cal's cheek
and silently flew away

Cal cried to himself
that night barely slept
when he awoke the next morning
he found himself adept

a new understanding
of what needed to be done
to save his fairy friends
from what he will become

He decided to ignore
the fairies requests for chit-chat
He locked all his windows
the fairies soon disappeared after that

And then Cal met a girl
and put the fairies out of mind
his new life beginning
leaving his old life behind

the fairies all smiled
as they watched him grow up

from deep in the shadows
they toasted their cups
to their friend, little Cal
who had learned the harsh truth
that fairies don't exist
except in your youth.

A poem to Beth on our wedding day

At this moment, I can see the future clearly
I can see us laughing, sharing our thoughts and dreams.
Sharing our lives.
Together, you and me facing the world.
I see us overcoming the bad times and
Savoring the good times.

At this moment, I feel like this is a beginning
None of the hurtful words
Or jealousy in our past matters
None of the sadness I have felt is presence
I can see us depending on each other
And learning to live in this new world.

At this moment, I don't believe I could breathe
Without you
You have become a part of my soul
A part that I could not live without
But this is not a sign of weakness
It is a sign of love.

This is the day I have been waiting for my whole life
This is my dream come true.

The ballad of Giovanni Contadino

In the simple days of yesteryear, it was refreshing when an amusing feel-good story like the one of Giovanni Contadino — an Italian shoe maker who mistook the Pope for a famous singer some 40 years ago — came along to entertain the masses.

Unlike today's headlines of infidelity involving Adam Levine and Liam Hemsworth, the 1970's headlines featured amazing, simple stories like the one of Contadino.

In sharp contrast to widespread political division being shoved down our throats in today's world, the 1970's public quickly became enamored of the wayward Italian, plying him with gifts and honorary titles and making him an international celebrity.

Washington Country Clerk Veronica Sawyer recently reminded me of the Contadino saga when she provided me with newspaper clippings on the incident and we had a good old time reminiscing about it.

The odyssey began for the 49-year-old Italian when his October 1969 train ride had to stop in a Vatican City train depot to refill the coal.

Only half-awake and apparently not having heard an earlier announcement that passengers would disembark in Vatican City during a brief stopover on their way to the Coliseum, Contadino went through the train depot, walked out of the building and into Saint Peter's square.

It was in Saint Peter's square that his amusing, heart-felt story took shape. In the square a large crowd of people were screaming and swaying from side to side. Contadino was curious what was going on and moved his way through the crowd and eventually saw a man singing in another language on a stage surrounded by security.

The singing man was dressed in what appeared to be a white jumpsuit decorated with rhinestones. Contadino didn't recognize any of the songs, but it was obvious in his mind that this was the American sensation, Elvis Presley.

Contadino became flustered and convinced himself that this was his one chance to become famous. If he could meet Elvis and impress him with his singing skills, he could become the international star he always dreamed he would be.

So, Contadino made his way to the front of the stage, addressed himself to the singing man and started singing as loud as he could. When he finished he was ushered off by the Vatican police and taken into custody.

It didn't take long before the media picked up on the story and Contadino became the international star he always wanted to be. For weeks he did television and newspaper interviews and was even offered cash for his story from a local filmmaker.

Eventually, the media picked up on another story involving a koala chewing bubble gum and left Contadino alone. No matter how hard Contadino tried to get back in the media, nothing worked. He eventually started drinking heavily and lost his business. 3 years later he committed suicide in Saint Peter's square, wearing a cardboard sign that said 'Good-bye Cruel world'.

And for a couple weeks Contadino was back in the news.

Into the Abyss / 7 Years

When the shadows come to take me
And I am no more
These words will be all that's left behind
For you to ignore

The memories, both unpleasant and great
Will both be explored
In the words that I will leave behind
Forevermore

With my pen against paper
My emotions will pour
Words to exchange
The body and soul that I wore
In the times before….

And the rhymes won't be perfect
For perfection, I deplored
Preferring instead,
The sweet imperfections that I bore

Each word I have written
On this day and those of yore
Have come from a place
Deeply hidden in my core

A void I have been trying to fill
Grasping for something more
Even when I thought it worthless
I wrote
Like it was my duty;
Albeit a chore

So without further ado
My ramblings shall commence
Enjoy or not,
I do not care
For these words shall be written
Without pretense

7 Years have passed since the feeling began
My spirit was crushed
broken and scattered into the wind
fleeting further and further away from me
until it was lost from my sight
Unable to recover
My Confidence gone
stolen

Inside a sadness blossoming
turning me into someone else
desires diminished
silent tears
feelings of

worthlessness
I became i

I had given up

7 long years I have lived as a nothing

Let it all out

"The test results are in"

Those are the only words I remember from the voice mail given to me by the little white box with the flashing red number 1.

I had waited all day for this call, nervous and scared. I tried going about my normal routine, but my mind would not let me complete a task. Be it reading a book, watching TV or vacuuming, everything led my mind back to the fear.
I remember crying a lot on that day.

I did my best to be strong for my 7 year old son, Joshua, who I had to take to school at 7:50am. He had a field day at the fire station on this day and had been excited about his special event. The contrast in our household bothered me all week. My husband and I agreed that it was best to go about our normal routine and not mention anything about my illness to my son.

So I put on my pretty face and acted my way through that morning. I remember wanting to break down and maybe even did at one point. However, I wiped my tears away and was strong for my son. He never noticed anything was wrong.

When I returned home I had noticed the red number 1 blinking on my answering machine. I ran toward the little white box and promptly pressed the shiny silver button.

"Honey, it's your Mom. I just wanted to make sure everything is ok. Please call me once you hear anything. My prayers are with you. Love you."

It was nice to hear her voice, but it wasn't the voice I wanted to hear. I know her intentions were good, but I had no patience on this day. All I wanted to hear on the other line of the phone was the hospital telling me that the results were negative.

Throughout the next hour I received six phone calls. Each of them from family members that wanted to wish me luck and to let me know their prayers are with me. Each of those phone calls was almost identical in words and in length. Each one made me feel a little more scared.

My husband called about 10 am. He told me that
he had a busy day, but would take off and wait
with me if I wanted him to. He tried to say all
the right words.
He tried to convince me that everything was
going to be ok and that we would celebrate this
weekend when the results come back negative.
He offered to take the rest of the day off four
times in the conversation, each time followed by
"but I don't really need to, since the test results
are going to be negative." I know he was trying
to be supportive, but he only made me more
scared. I wanted
desperately for him to come home, but instead
replied four times "It's ok. Stay at work and get
your mind off of it. I will be ok."

At 11:35 I received a call from the school. They
let me know that my son's lunch was
"accidentally destroyed" and wanted to know if I
could drop something off for him at the local fire
station. I told them I could.

I fixed my make-up, made his lunch and drove
10 miles to the fire station. I wiped the tears
from my face when I parked in the parking lot
and walked through the over-sized doors in
front. I gave the lunch bag to a woman sitting at
a desk right next to the door. The bag had my

son's name on it and I explained to her the situation, which she already knew. In the background I could see the children standing next to a fire truck, listening to a fireman explain all of the gadgets on the fire engine. I could see Joshua standing there with a smile on his face. He was so interested in the fire engine that he didn't even notice me waving at him.

I drove back home with my son's picture in my mind. I thought about him growing up in the world without me. I could picture his graduation, his marriage and his children. The tears flowed heavily.

When I got home I noticed the red number 1 blinking on the answering machine. I slowly made my way to the little white box and pressed the shiny silver button again.

"The test results are in"

Some days

some days the waves
wash over me
darkness starts to takes control
as i struggle to breathe
as i struggle to find the want
or need
to live
within my soul

some nights, i do not want to fight
i want to give in
give up
let the darkness win
begin again on the other side
and for a minute i let myself sink
i can see the beautiful bottom
i reach out and want to touch it
to let it consume me
fully

some days I find hope
warmth washing over me
as I smile
watching the lives we created
the home we made

the happiness
the love

some nights, I want to fall in your arms
and begin a new
change my pathology,
begin my metamorphosis
leave the darkness behind

some days i watch you struggle
with the same disease
neither of us speaking the truth
as we dive down into sadness

some nights i feel lost
we are divided
caught in our own webs of despair
separated by unspoken words

some days the waves
wash over me...

Song of Songs

It isnt the disease, as much as the cure
You can never go back, once you are lured
never get back, that sense of being pure
you might think Im right, but Im not so sure

It isnt the race, as much as the end
you can never be happy, once you pretend
never be happy, once you descend
I might be right, but I cant comprehend

It isnt the love, as much as the familiarity
the comfort you find, in that clarity
the comfort you find, is a rarity
to prove this theory, trade for solidarity

It isnt the faith, as much as the dream
you will find the truth, will never redeem
the truth, will only agleam
I hope Im wrong, but that is the scheme

It isnt the pain, as much as the isolation
the loneliness that lingers, becomes a fixation
the loneliness lingers, until liberation
Its been that way, since the beginning of
creation...

For the children

Peaceful in my bed, illuminated by the suns
corona,
When news came in from Oklahoma,
A powerful message, to change our nations
course,
Caused me to seek out the source

I came across Murder, on my way,
He resembled a man named Lindsay,
A crooked smile, yet confident;
As six blood-hounds followed his death-like
scent:

All were gorged; fat with greed,
Not afraid to plant their seed,

For one vote, two vote, ends in six,
The nation mourns, the dark eclipse

For which the belief in faith did grow.

Following closely, I met fraud,
A Triumphant noise, the crowds applaud;
His lies believed, for he lied well,
Even when his kingdom fell.

And the children born of sin,
In poverty, with their broken kin,
Single mothers hold the blame,
Branded leeches, they proclaim!

Armed with the Bible, and a gun,
Dividing the nation with their "truth",
Shoot your neighbor, just for fun,
Kick them in their tooth!

And many more school shootings came,
In this "ghastly masquerade",
Let them die, it's our god given right,
No peaceful sleep for the kids tonight.

Next my friend Sir Anarchy:
he followed closely by,
With a spritz of naïveté,
He blinded innocent eyes;
His shine like diamonds, cool and crisp,
Bringing forth the Apocalypse.

The disgraced leader wore a royal crown;
In his castle Mar-a-lago;
Shouting out across the land,
'I AM THE CHOSEN ONE, LETS GO!"

His campaign, kept moving on,

Despite the indictments, or the proven con,
Shredding the constitution with his lies,
With no care who lives or dies.

And the states made their morality laws,
To protect the children from their flaws,
Screaming "let those who are different die!"
Be they gay, or trans, or bi.

And the confidence it flowed so red,
Like blood stains streaked across their bed,
God complex, they blew their flutes,
When they cashed the checks of the destitute.
And that in turn paid for prostitutes.

In smaller towns, the rhetoric spreads,
From bar to bar, from bed to bed,
The fear infects the Ignorant mind,
Hatred is born, and it shines

Each peaceful citizen, is scared to death,
Terror in each heartbeat, and each breath,
And when their candidate does succeed,
They rejoice, as the children bleed!

And still the crowds they followed their king,
The songs of Judas, they did sing,
In a most unironic way,
No ounce of awareness of their hypocrisy,

We have waited, for the economy to heal,
Yet the government continues to steal,
In the name of the children, they exclaim,
And redirect the blame.

Words like liberal, and the right,
We're cautioned, and we were prepared to fight,
The enemy that was born to destroy,
The other side will steal our joy.

Ruin the reputation of our teachers,
Inclusion is the evil way,
Listen to the disgraced preachers,
As they spread their disguised hate,

And as the drones drop bombs abroad,
We listen to their words of fraud,
Misdirection, in the truest form,
As we play along, divisions born.

Lies are told, with evidence,
Conceived with evil precedence,
Stories made up, to share their tale,
The make believe will always prevail.

And neighbors become our enemies,
They are sinful entities,
The state anoints us to intercede,

For the children, make them bleed.

We're taught, or brainwashed, to believe,
The other side is there to deceive,
Their villain ways need to be stopped,
They give us guns, so we can drop.

In Gods name I beg and plead,
For you to stop and join me,
Turn away from the voices loud,
For the children, make us proud.

Put down your guns, be open to learn,
Conversations will help you turn,
That hate into love, it's not that hard,
It's up to you to flip the card.

I curse the heavens

I curse the heavens,
The sky, the stars!
Take back the prayers,
That caused my scars,
Erase the tattoo burned on my skin,
The remembrance of my solemn sin,
The ink they used, it seeped inside,
Tainting my blood, my wicked mind,
Until all I could do was hide.

I curse the fates, my destiny,
I can't concede to be, the me, it sees,

I've been blessed with a rebel heart,
And want to tear their pages apart,
Tomorrow may have been written, but not by my
hand,
I won't follow their script, do you understand?

15 things I can never tell you

15 things I can never tell you
15 things you'll never know
15 things that I keep hidden
15 things I will never show
Signs are found in words I speak
Evidence in my glances, leaked
If you could unearth my darkest heart
I would share my deepest parts
Decipher me with silent stares
In quiet moments, with just us there
Decode my inner policies
And I will give you everything
For I am only half a soul
These hidden lies, they only grow
And each day I become
Further from an honest love
It pains me deep this web I spin
These 15 things I hold within
These 15 things I cannot tell
Bound me in this brutal hell
I wish to tell, I wish to scream
These 15 things I wish redeemed
Unvoiced deceit, still I hide
These 15 things, I keep inside
15 things I can never tell you

15 things you'll never know
15 things that I keep hidden
15 things I will never show

Ghost

Whispers of the words you spoke,
Vibrate in my lucid mind,
Visible like wisps of smoke,
The reason has been undefined.

Cautious with your aberration,
You disappeared without a trace,
With no obvious explanation,
My entire existence has been displaced.

This wasn't simply a trick of light,
The whispered words they cut too deep,
Nor am I blessed with the gift of sight,
There's another answer in which I seek.

It wasn't a dream, for that I am sure,
Your image was all too real,
What I knew to be true, I must abjure,
The pain of loss, I must finally allow myself to
feel.

The wish of my life

When I was a child
I found a golden key in the motionless grass
It held secrets beyond my comprehension
With clues hidden in both the future
And in the past

In my childish mind
All I could see was it's shiny gold skin
I was blinded to the possibilities it held
Deep within

And so I sold the golden key
To the first to offer cash
I gave them my gift
For something that won't last

Blame it on innocence
For that's what I did
I offered that excuse
When judged for my sins

But from the moment I sold the key
And the money touched my hand
My mind opened up
And I could understand

Instantly knowing
That I would regret
Trading the golden key
For each day I had left.

When we're old

In the twilight of our years
When we're old and gray
And our children have left the nest
Leaving us with empty days

I'll be there to remind you
How much I cherished this life
I appreciate how we got each other through
The toughest days of strife

How lucky we were, the night that we met
To find our true romance
It hasn't always been easy, but I loved each day
I'll say that in advance

For I know it'll never change,
The love we share will only grow,
And I would be fully satisfied
If that's the only love I'll ever know

Inside

In 1990, when my emotions burned
with the intensity of volcanic lava
and my hormones raged like a violent storm
I was drugged and caged like a wild animal

They starved me, made me weak
And tried to put words in my mouth
Pills of poison forced down my throat
Requiring me to show them proof that I
swallowed

My mind and body were sound
But the gaslighting commenced
Trying to convince me that I had gone mad

Scratching words in sterile furniture
So other kids wouldn't feel so alone
I refused to let them have control

I quickly learned to hide pills under my tongue,
spitting them out in the toilet when the nurses
left
Luckily I saw the cameras pointed at the seat
and found ways to dispose of them with regular
bathroom routines

I listened to stories of violent and suicidal kids,
watching them leave the hell before I did, some
of them died before I ever had a chance to meet
them in the real world

And eventually I was released and thrown back
into the world, missing the trust I had before I
entered. I had missed half of my senior year and
lost contact with friends, changing my life
forever.

Bicycle

Invited to the lions den
Told to bring my younger friends
We were special
We were seen
Riding our bicycles to the obscene

White cotton collar in a black uniform
Gave him automatic trust,
misused with the sins he did perform
He declared himself a god
Drunk on lust

A thief, he thrived
As he moved from parish to parish
Spreading his disease
And leaving a body count in his path,
Yet to the church he was cherished

The kids that spoke up and shared their stories
We're branded with the letter L
And forced to apologize publicly
To the devil, in their own hell

For years and years his violence won
And he was not the only one
Millions of kids were finally believed
When it was finally said and done

Gloom

Flowers bloom
In my impending doom
The contrast is enduring

The darkened room
Where the love illumes
I can finally feel the curing

Hope is a curious thing
You never know what it will bring

And at the alter I will know…

Am I living or am I dead?
What are these visions
That dance through my head?
Who speaks the voices
That cry out in pain?

Who is there? Who is there?

I cry out in silence
My words reflected
Back into my senses

I become disoriented
And faint into the darkness
Memories float around me
Taunting me
Making me remember
That day

The day I swore
I would forget
The only regret
I've ever had

The voices become louder
And I know
What I have to do
To stop them
But I know
I'm not that strong

Still I try
With all my soul
Yet I stop myself
And force myself to live life

And at the alter I will know...

The price of freedom

I keep waiting for peace
In the midst of a war
I refuse to wear their uniform
Believing that somehow it will keep me from
fighting

I welcome my enemy to my table
Offering conversation
And love

Both sides keep arguing
Either ignoring me
Or hating me
Calling me names
Threatening me with violence
As I stand there with open arms

I can't protect myself from the bullets
Their weapons penetrate
Deeply
Causing pain, but not regret
I won't change course
I cannot change course

My morality guides me

Born a mediator I don't know how to fight
My open hands
Welcome
Never closed in fists

I may not trust people
But I never expect the hatred they bring
I cannot grasp
How the inability to understand differences
Triggers loathing

On the edge

My experiences have taught me nothing
As I don't have the answers still
The only thing I've learned so far
Is nil

My mind tends to speak in cursive
In a language most can't understand
With words formed in shapes and colors
Meanings barely at my command

My path has gone through woods and rivers
By myself most of the way
As I look back, I realize
It was the only route that I could take

United States in 2023

Aging millionaires, posed as politicians
Rule with a wicked hand
In contempt of our country, they lead with
division
Pushing down those, that dare to stand

Rulers, with not an ounce of compassion
Vampire-like with their unsustainable greed
Sucking on the lifeblood of my people
Who are starved and broken, left to bleed

A growing military, to "protect the globe"
Sanguine with their promises of peace
As our drones drop bombs upon those
We are trying to save, the war will never cease

Religion, devoid of the message of Christ
Godless in their hateful endeavors
The senate attempts their biggest heist
To steal the country, they think they're clever

Their conceit may be their undoing
Although the states have been torn asunder
The youth, with their inclusionist dreams
Could be the glue, to wake us from our
slumber…